I0620483

Bad Fruit
Copyright © 2025 Jerry T. Johnson

Cover Art by Matthew DeGroat @apothekapress
Author Photo by Matthew Hupert

The font used is Century Schoolbook
The cover fonts are Paabaaliot and custom lettering

All rights reserved. No duplication or reuse of any selection is
allowed without the express written consent of the publisher.

Gnashing Teeth Publishing
242 East Main Street
Norman AR 71960
http://GnashingTeethPublishing.com

Printed in the United States of America

ISBN 978-1-966075-12-7

Non-Fiction: Poetry

Gnashing Teeth Publishing First Edition

Praise for *Bad Fruit*

Poet Jerry Johnson's *Bad Fruit* is a dynamic, provocative, and well-crafted collection of contemporary poetry, completely captivating from start to finish. Johnson exhibits innovation and poetic prowess as he explores themes of beauty and joy while "dancing" to a steady influx of friction and toxicity driven by both capitalism and racism. Throughout, Johnson uses lyrical rhythm and precise language to punch up the tension of his braided themes. Included are two particularly significant longer pieces that vibrate with intensity. "The Race" is an extraordinary compressed 400-year history of the ongoing challenges in the fight for equality and inclusion, written in first-person narrative perspective. "November 22nd, 1963" is an excellent lengthy poem capturing a loss of innocence of a young boy and the US simultaneously, as news of JFK's assassination spreads across the nation and into the narrator's grade school and family home. A consistently remarkable collection, highly recommended.

Kat Georges, author, *Awe and Other Words Like Wow*

Jerry Johnson's latest collection takes on all the hard things: gun violence, political corruption, the lasting impact of racism, the atrocities of war, and environmental destruction where "birds plunge from the sky while flying/ in bad air cooked by your burning smokestacks." It's a collection that rages, even as it takes responsibility, even as it makes us culpable for the world's horrors. It's a wake-up call, a cry in the darkness. There is hope here, but when he writes that "I compartmentalize my shaky/nerves into my own baggage," we know ourselves in that "I." These powerful poems demand we pay attention and do something.

Laurel S. Peterson, Poet Laureate, Norwalk, CT 2016 – 2019, Author of *Daughter of Sky* and *Do You Expect Your Art to Answer?*

Jerry Johnson's book of poems *Bad Fruit* is a deep exposition
of this world so full of injustice, oppression, and racial inequity,
and while it gets harder to not fall from the tree full of one in the same
here poet Johnson passes along something ripe for understanding and
fruitful to the mind
as he continues to explore, inspire, and keep on dancing.

Peter Carlaftes, *Life in the Past Lane*

Bad Fruit

Table of Contents

Bad Fruit

shriveled orange skins
black and blue limes
purple apples, black pears
rotted bananas, saddened
grapes, withered figs.
bad fruit   served daily
at breakfast, at lunch
at dinner, at midnight
during the late night
snacking fridge raid.
lately all we been eating
is bad fruit. we spread
the table in the morning.
with proper etiquette
we hold our knives and
our forks. we bite, we
chew, we swallow. later
our guts rebel. we hug
stools. violently we puke.
we become plague, we
become pestilence, we
become pandemic, we
become epidemic, slowly
we become   bad fruit

Until All The Cows Come Home

folk broadcast bull over airwaves
all day long until all the cows come
home and Malcolm said *the chickens*
come home to roost and Malcolm is
gone but not forgotten and Martin is gone
but not forgotten and Emmett Till still
weeps and blood still runs deep in
Langston's Rivers and the liars no longer
tell little white lies, now loud liars yell
loud lies – shamelessly – all day long til
all the cows come home and the chickens
still come home to roost and shame flees
scenes of crosses burning and truth has been
declared public enemy number one and love
has been declared public enemy number two
and compassion has been captured and sentenced
to death and civility and sensibility are on the run
being hunted down all day long by a posse of cowards
all day long until the cows come home, all day long, all
day long, all day long, all day long and the chickens
still come home to roost

Feed The Bull

feed the bull. mate
bull mate, make money.
feed the cow. milk cow milk,
make babies. beg the hen.
egg hen egg, feed masses,
crow rooster crow. slop
the hogs so greedy and so
the pigs greedy, so greedy
whose not greedy. swing
cleaver – butcher. butcher,
butcher make bacon, chew
the fat, scale balance sheets.
calculate, recalculate income
statements. slap yourself silly
when numbers don't add up.
elevator, elevator hurry. I need to
leave ivory towers. crow rooster,
cackle hen, grunt hog, snort bull.
this ain't no Animal Farm
I'm leaving ivory towers

Rush Hour

subways and metro trains
and shuttle buses and
taxis and ride shares
and schedules and
on time arrivals and
late arrivals and reading
while riding and sleeping
while riding and oversleeping
missing your stop and
rescheduling and rearranging
your day and rearranging
your life and miles and
miles day after day and
wear and tear and tear and
wear and stress for the weary
and smiles and frowns and
grimaces and smirks and tears
and payday and paying bills
and paying bills and days off
and overtime again and paying
bills and paying bills and overtime
again and roadblocks and stalled
engines and trees falling on your
railroad tracks and paying bills
and paying bills and morning rush
and five p.m. deadlock and evening
and night and midnight and paying
bills and paying bills and alarm
clocks screaming   early every morning

Cruising At High Altitude

shake, shake, shake
the airplane shakes as it
lifts off from the steamy
runway. knock, rock and roll
bang the luggage in the
overhead compartments.

I compartmentalize my shaky
nerves into my own baggage
claim where all my drama's stored.
my airplane climbs. I lean back,
I let myself feel the mild g-force
press me. press me g-force,
press me.

I relax in my g-force pressure
and I ride the climb into a blue
sky adorned with pillowy clouds
bearing pleasant friendly smiles.
the skies are not frowning at
humans today.

my airplane levels at cruising
altitude. I myself level, calm,
steady. my plane is high, I am
as high as my plane because
I left all my troubles down on the
earth below and I cruise at my
mellowed altitude and I cruise at
my mellowed attitude and for a
moment in my daze — I dance.

Toxicity

my eyes water and burn every time you open
your mouth at a press conference or in a news
interview or during one of your filibusters.
your words are toxic fumes of
mixing bleach and ammonia.
.

the cyanide smell of bitter almonds.
my nostrils swell from irritation your
deceit, your false claims, irritation your incessant
misrepresentation. I gag and puke, your words stink,
your words are the bitter almond.

salmon and trout choke and float in murky
waters disturbed by waste pissed from lies.
birds plunge from the sky while trying to fly
in bad air cooked by your burning smokestacks
puffing your loony, vitriolic broadcasts.

you scoff at global warming, you enable
irresponsible factories, you cut funding to
control emissions, you take the stage and
ridicule all the warnings and you tear down
all the danger signs. you are the toxic,
you are the perpetuating lie, you are
the toxicity in a toxic, toxic, toxic world.

Monsters

monsters dressed in monstrous
garments, welcomed into our homes
for dinner, seated at the head of our
tables, knife in one hand, gun in the
other. eyes dark, lifeless, bloodthirsty.
teeth bared in lying smiles, mouth busy,
lips moving —rapidly. affectionately,
we gaze at the monsters. spellbound
by their grandiosity, mesmerized by
their grandiloquence we applaud and
reward with standing ovations. aroused,
we lust for violence and riot. maddened
we abhor peace, we raise our middle
finger to diplomacy. and the monsters
grin beholding us as we become mobs
as we unleash our rabid dog as we knot
our hangman rope, as we sharpen our
own knives, as we load our own guns,
as we too become monsters.

The Dancer

lately, I've been dancing
on all my tears   without slip
or fall   —every Plier I've bended,
every Entendre I've stretched,
every Relever I rose, every
Glisser I would glide, every
Sauter I jumped, every Elancer
I darted, every Tourner I turned.

my dance floor is drenched in tears
and still I dance and still I maintain
my balance. lightning strikes, flash
in my skies while thunder cracks.
I dance with the lightning, and I roll
to the drums of the thunder. There are
no raindrops falling from the clouds,
for my grief is my cloud and my teardrops
are my rainstorms.

Suddenly, earth stands still. I do not fall,
I stand still. earth then quakes, I'm still
standing and again I start to dance.
and my grief plays on and the lightning
flashes on and the thunder rolls on and
my teardrops still fall,   yet I refuse
to stop   — dancing.

Liberators

a low ceiling of clouds and mist envelops my aircraft
I can't see the ground, I can't see the airport, can't see
treetops, just cloud and mist, cloud and mist   suddenly
in the midst emerges   a tall spire   both gothic and
baroque   an immense ziggurat standing sentinel,
watching our every move,   watching our entry
into Warsaw airspace. it is the Ministry of Science
and Culture, not so affectionately known as
"Stalin's Wedding Cake."

it is Sunday, June fifth, nineteen ninety-four. one day
before the Fiftieth Anniversary of D-Day. Also my arrival
date for my first European assignment. I look at Stalin's
Wedding Cake, his gift to a city razed by fury of Third Reich
madmen while a Red Army just stood afar, across the
Wisła and watched the rage, the madness, the slaughter
then marched over, trampling through the ruin declaring
themselves   Liberators

Liberators of Poland
Liberators of Estonia
Liberators of Lithuania
Liberators of Czechoslovakia
Liberators of Belarus
Liberators of Ukraine

Liberators draped in iron curtains
Liberators bearing chains
Liberators wearing barbed wire
Liberators erecting chained link fence
Liberators forecasting A Cold War Winter
Liberators trampling freedom underfoot   again

Graffiti

origin: mid 19th century; from Italian (plural), from graffio 'a scratch' (New Oxford American Dictionary)

itchy is that wall
as it awaits graffio.

the graffitist,
urban artist,
revolutionary
—pushing back

against norms,
challenging tradition,
fostering change.

revisionist of the street
you share your thoughts
with us —the concrete,

the steel, the asphalt,
the bridges long, the
freight cars wide,
the skylines tall.

your hieroglyphs, tell a story.
your symbols represent.
notes scratched on sheet music
your clefs set pitch to song.

itchy are the walls
that await the graffio
of the graffitist.

The Lost Hour

I got to bed late last night, the clocks sprang forward,
I slept through all our dreams.

the world nearly ended and I was not available to
rescue our world from violence.

a war started and I missed the draft and the call to action,
I never committed to gun or sword.

the earth quaked but I slept through the tremor, I snored
through terror and aftermath.

bombs fell, mushrooms rose but I did not stir during the blast
nor did I rise after the fallout.

the polar cap melted, icebergs floated into sounds and harbors
I turned over and farted.

pestilence, epidemic and pandemic ravished grandmothers
      leaving
bereaved grandchildren,

a gavel banged on a sound block. in the months of June and
July snow covered the equator,

a gavel banged on the sound block. rusted ships spilled oil into
      gulfs
the storms came, levees broke,

neighborhoods became flood. a gavel banged on the sound block,
the house was called to order

I sat up, my eyes still closed the bills were presented,
it was time to take a vote.

a gavel banged on the sound block

Remains

my world tossed by turbulence rattles
and shakes. my ceilings cast hail, my
basements drop into hell and disaster
calls me on my cell phone greeting me
with "Hello" and "this is nine one-one
calling you —and you are about to
have an emergency." My neighborhood
explodes into stabbings and shootings
and robberies and theft and graft and
lying politicians and creepy creeps
creeping into bedrooms, creepy creeps
creeping into boardrooms, creepy creeps
creeping into bank accounts and the assaults
and the assaults and the stealing and the
stealing and the rich remain the rich and
the help remain the help, and the slaves remain
the slaves and the poor remain the poor and
fools remain fools and idiots remain idiots
and liars remain liars and thieves remain thieves
and murderers remain murderers and the murdered
remain murdered and the slaughtered remain

slaughtered.

Yekaterinburg

September, Nineteen Ninety-Six
Yekaterinburg, Russia. two degrees
Celsius, about thirty-five Fahrenheit.

eight of us sitting in the restaurant
a little after midnight, sipping hot
coffee and throat burning vodka,

just trying to stay warm.
"We do not turn the furnaces on
until October," the hotel manager said.

our rooms felt frozen, therefore we
stayed close to the kitchen where
heat emanated from the cook stoves.

I watched the steam rise from my cup.
l thought about the start of that day,
that first morning ride to the office.

twenty minutes into our journey, we
passed by a wide lake. mounted near
its edge sat a large white sculpture
absorbing the rays of a chilly day's sun
—glistening.

Anatoly, our driver, spoke. "nearby is
the spot where the Romanov's were
executed." hushed and silenced we

were, our imaginations violated by
flashes of history, of bayonets, of
screams, of gunfire, of blood.

I sipped my brew as my mind returned
to the dining room. "Last call for the
kitchen," the kitchen manager said.
we paid our tabs, went to our rooms.
my room was huge, it was quite cold.
fully clothed, I went to bed, my blankets
—a cocoon.

a fight broke out in the room next to mine.
I heard loud voices and crying and shattering
of glass and pounding against the wall.
the violence subsided, I fell asleep.

the Bolsheviks, the Romanovs visited
my dreams. flashes of history, flashes
of gunfire, bloodstained glint of bayonets,
sounds of rage, sounds of screams.

Yekaterinburg

Melancholy

melancholy, disoriented,
my last nerve unraveling,
my earth quaking, my skies
always a disappointing gray,
terror wakes me every morning,
monsters put me to bed at night,
I scream from the horror of another
midnight nightmare dream.

all my hopes are dashed by
constant threats, all my variables
collide, toxicity blows fallout
all over my aspirations and I can't
breathe and I can't weep anymore
because I'm all dried up of tears.

I try to be brave, courageous but
I regress into all my fears. monsters
still put me to bed at night. terror
still wakes me early in the morning,
I want to binge on jars of vodka mixed
with bourbon from sunrise to sundown
but I pause and I refrain.

I want to swallow, choke down bottles
of quaaludes from sunrise to sundown
but I pause and I refrain. I want stand
on a ledge incessantly howling at the
stars, at the moon, at the sun, at the
earth from sunrise to sundown, but
stilled —I pause and I refrain.

An Unexpected Reprieve

I'm parched from heat and lack of water,
the soles of my boots feel like they're melting.
sweat runs down my forehead into my eyes,
my skin is peeling from the burn of the sun.

the handle of my shovel breaks my callouses,
I bleed. Soon I will have new callouses.
scars on my back elicit stares from my
friends and fears from my enemies.

the field that I work in fights against me,
it does not yield to my strike or my strength.
my bones ache, my muscles inflamed, my
sinews torn. Yet, I do not limp, though my

body is assaulted, my mind and composure
are strong. I am resolved not to bend or break
under the pressure of antagonists who
desire to keep me chained under the whip
of a merciless sun.

suddenly a cool breeze happens, giving
me relief, shortly thereafter clouds appear,
soft thunder claps and a heavy rain falls,
the soil I was hired to plow softens.

I'm happy for the downpours. I find shelter
from the storm, I sit, I let my bones, my
muscles, my body relax. I sigh a sigh of
relief — I laugh at my antagonists.

I'm thankful for the reprieve of the coolness
of the breeze and the help of the batter of the rain,
and I stand   and I dance.

The Race

"...You do not take a person who, for years, has been hobbled by chains and liberate him, bring him up to the starting line of a race and then say, 'you are free to compete with all the others,' and still justly believe that you have been completely fair... "

**President Lyndon B. Johnson, June 4th, 1965
- Howard University Commencement**

four hundred years ago a race —in progress.
a race —for freedom, a race —for what
eventually would be called the American Dream.
I was not allowed —to run in it.

I asked if I could sign up —and viciously
I was lashed with tongue and whip
for my uppity n-word notion. The race
was on but forbidden was I —to contend.

destined I was for the cotton fields.
destined l was for the mops and
the brooms. destined I was for
the shovels and the ditches.
destined I was, so I was told.

Juneteenth, officially free, granted forty acres
and a mule. I thought I had a chance to run
the race, but then eighteen seventy-seven
compromise was passed

opening the door for Nathan Bedford Forrest
and his cross burning, pointy-hood wearing
night riders, opening the doors for Jim Crow
whose laws trampled down my dreams the more.

turn of the twentieth century, a few things
changed. The second Industrial Revolution
neared its end. I was allowed entry into
another race —the Olympics. I ran, I won,
putting Aryan superiority to shame.

Then came World War Two. Tuskegee
Graduate, I flew war planes. I was a hero.
I gained other skills and my education
increased the more.

After the Olympics and after the war
I attempted to sign up for the race
and again I was forbidden.

meanwhile, I found a path onto
the racetrack. unregistered and
unofficial I ran. I discovered plasma,
I discovered many uses of the peanut.

On my own with no recognition, I ran
and I invented and I discovered but
still I was limited from inventing
and discovering more   falling further
behind the other runners in the race.

the nineteen fifties came. and I spoke up.
I marched, I protested —peacefully,
and I was beaten, but I did not hit back.
dogs were ordered to maul me,

but I did not fight back. unjustly I was
jailed but I did not violently revolt.
I was gunned down by assassins
but I did not shoot back.

the nineteen sixties, I was finally allowed
to run the race. But I was so far behind
all the other runners, who had hundreds of
years of head-start.

laws and directives were passed to give
me a fighting chance, to balance the
playing field, to make the race fair,
And so I ran.

through snide remarks about quotas I ran.
through innuendo that certainly I was not
capable to do the work, I ran. and I ran and
I ran and I ran and I succeeded!

But it still is not enough. Today, I'm still
hundreds of years behind. the laws and
directives passed in the sixties now struck down.

And with straight face the courts now say
we are all equal.   But in this race for the
American Dream. —treated equal –we are not.

November 22nd, 1963

eleven twenty-two p.m. November
twenty-second the year twenty
twenty-two. It's my birthday,
don't ask my age, let's just say

I've traveled miles and miles
and miles   and yes I bear a little
wear and tear but I'm fortunate
my wear and tear is minimal.

It's November twenty-second,
twenty twenty-two but my thoughts
travel to November twenty-second
nineteen sixty-three, my eighth birthday.

I remember that morning's walk
to Washington School in Greenville,
South Carolina. back then It was
called a Negro school   the word

Negro   a big improvement over
the word Colored and so much
better than the other N-word.

I remember that morning walk,
seven-thirty a.m.   Mickey Mike
Portman, Anthony Mark Robinson
and I met at our usual spot on

Old Paris Mountain Road across
the street from the concrete,
cement and asphalt mixing plant.
entering the plant we walked down

the railroad tracks passing mounds
and mounds of gray gravel, mounds of
sand glistening beneath sunbeams,
no clouds the sky a warm light blue.

"Mickey Mike, you got the bag?"
"Yes Anthony, I got the bag"
we scoured the tracks and grass
we found the cigarette butts

we stuffed the cigarette butts
into Mickey Mike's brown
paper bag, "You know we've
never seen the Green Lady."

"Just because we never saw her,
don't mean a thing. I don't want
to be eaten, you Anthony? you
Roger? I don't want to be eaten."

second grade school legend warned
second graders to Beware of the
Green Lady.   She hung out around
the railroad tracks looking for children

walking to school and if the children
had no cigarette butts she would eat
the children, therefore, we always kept
an extra lunch bag of cigarette butts
for the Green Lady.

we walked, we made progress, no
Green Lady seen or heard. but then
we heard sledge hammers driving
metal spikes into railroad ties.

we saw black and white stripes
on shirts, black and white stripes
on hats, black and white stripes on
pants worn by black men chained

one to another   lined up and down
the tracks smoking cigs slinging
hammers that sang that Sam Cooke
song, "Chain Gang" and clink,

clink, clink sounded the movement
of their feet when they sidestepped
from one rail tie to the other and

clack, clack, clack went the cock of rifles
held by the guards and pumped were
the shotguns ready for bloodshed
just in case any prisoner got out of line.

We left the railroad tracks and
walked down a path through
a wooded area, our eyes peeled,
for the Green Lady.

our path led us out of the woods
spilling onto Loop Street right in
front of Washington School.

"Anthony, Anthony put the bag
of butts under that bush there. "
"Mickey Mike there is no Green
Lady" "Just hide the bag, just

hide the bag, Anthony," Anthony
stood still. "Roger, we have never

seen the Green Lady" I sighed,
"Anthony, just hide the bag."

Upon entry into our classroom
our second grade teacher,
Ms. Ramsey led the class in
singing Happy Birthday to me.

Afterwards we proceeded with
our lessons of the day. Lunchtime,
most grabbed their lunch bags,
some ate in the cafeteria.

After lunch, it was rest for thirty
minutes and then recess. We
loved recess. we loved to play
kickball during recess.

kickball we played, much like
soccer we kicked the round ball
and much not like soccer we ran
with the ball clutched in our hands.

the bell rang, recess over, back to
class we went. Our lessons resumed.
one-thirty p.m. Eastern Standard Time,
gunshots rang out in Dallas, Texas.

Two p.m. Eastern Standard Time
in the midst of our afternoon
lessons, we take a second recess

"Anthony, why are we taking a
second recess?" "Roger, I don't know.
Mickey Mike is bringing the kick ball"
"Yeah, Anthony, we get to play

kickball again, Yeah, kickball."
Mickey Mike arrived without
the kickball. "Mickey Mike,
where is the kickball?"

"I left it in the classroom.
Ms. Ramsey was crying,
Ms. Martin was with her,
Ms. Martin was crying too.

They said the President
was shot. Shot in the head."
"Don't say that Mickey Mike."
"I'm just saying what they said"

The bell rang, back to the class
we were summoned. Ms. Ramsey
dried her eyes as we entered
her classroom and took our seats.

then Ms. Ramsey looked at us,
tears welling in her eyes again,
"School is closed for the day.
The President was shot in Dallas.
Everybody go home."

Mickey Mike, Anthony and I
walked back down the railroad
tracks. the Chain Gang was gone.
We'd forgotten the cigarette butts.

We'd forgotten the Green Lady
We'd forgotten kickball and all.
We did not forget Ms. Ramsey,
Ms. Martin and their tears.

We were silent most of the journey
We reached the cement, asphalt
and concrete mixing plant, "Roger,
Mickey Mike, Nobody's working"

"Yeah, Anthony, Nobody's working."
back down Old Paris Mountain Road
we walked, we split up at the corner
of Earnhardt, I walked into the house

The television was on, my Father
watched. My Father was silent.
I looked at the television. The
reporters were very sad, the

network went from the reporters
to scenes in Dealey Plaza, banners
and flags laid on the ground. men,
women crying, faces cupped in hands.
.
shocked, I was.   the President died.
"Boy, don't just stand there like a statue,
put your school books away. Your Mama
will be home soon. Nobody's working."

I put my school books away, went back
to the living room, my Father silent
I was silent too. We watched T.V.
in silence. my Mama arrived.

my Mama was sad, "Do they know
who shot the President?"
"They arrested this Oswald guy."
"Who's that?" "Don't know."

Large white borders appeared
on our black and white television
"Oh, oh," my Daddy said, "Oh, oh,"
my Mama said, "No!" I thought

The white borders disappeared,
the television screen went black
a thin white horizontal line displayed
in the middle of the screen, flickered

and pop went the cathode ray tube.
"It's gone," my Daddy said, "It's gone,"
my Mama said. I didn't say anything.
"I'll pick up a new T.V. tomorrow."

"Mama, can I go to Mickey Mike's
house? I want to watch the news."
"No, Roger, just stay home with us."

my mind leaves nineteen sixty-three
and returns to the present November
twenty-second, twenty twenty-two
at eleven twenty-two p.m.

I thought about that day,
The President had been shot,
The President dying. I thought
about Ms. Ramsey, Ms. Martin,
an entire nation crying.

I thought about Anthony,
Mickey Mike and myself.
we were just second graders
who collected cigarette butts
for the mythical Green Lady,

who loved walking between
the mounds of gravel and sand
at the cement, concrete and asphalt
mixing plant, just second graders who
loved playing kickball during recess

we were just second graders
enjoying our days of innocence
an innocence violated by scenes
of chained men in chain gangs

an innocence violated by armed
guards bearing shotguns pumped
with shells and rifles cocked
with bullets.

an innocence violated by
assassination and murder
committed by a hatred and a hate
we were too young to understand.

I'm much older than eight years
old now, my innocence long gone
and on one hand I do and on the
other hand, I still do not — understand.

Driving Through My Last Winter Storm

driving through my last winter storm
just a few more miles to go

before sunshine and blue skies,
before daffodils and honeybees,
before cherry blossoms and
black-capped chickadees

driving through my last winter storm
just a few more miles to go

before peace and love, before lost
civility found, before mending
of broken hearts

before homeless
noticed, before hungered
fed, before naked clothed,
before the frozen melts

before all the liars are
exposed, before all the
lost and stolen are restored

driving through my last winter storm,
my last mile before Spring unfolds,
when brides and grooms anticipate,
when thrush and nightingale sing

Acknowledgements

South Carolina Bards (2022 Anthology) - Driving Through My Last Winter Storm

Three Rooms Press (Maintenant 16, 2022) – Toxicity

Three Rooms Press (Maintenant 17, 2023) – Liberators South Carolina Bards (2023 Anthology) – Rush Hour

Last Leaves – Bad Fruit

Poetry Americana -- Until All The Cows Come Home

Flora Fiction – Graffiti

Three Rooms Press (Maintenant 18, 2024) – Feed the Bull

South Carolina Bards (2024 Anthology) – Remains

Obsidian: Literature & Arts in the African Diaspora – Yekaterinburg

Floral Fiction – The Dancer

Eastern Sea Bards (2024 Poetry Anthology) – Cruising At High Altitude

About the Author

Jerry T Johnson is a Poet and Spoken Word Artist whose poetry
has appeared in a variety of literary publications worldwide.
Jerry is author of 2 poetry collections: *A Coldness* published by
Finishing Line Press and *Poets Should Not Write About Politics*
by Evening Street Press. His poetry collection *Poets Should Not
Write About Politics* was selected winner of the Evening Street
Press' 2020 Sinclair Poetry prize and his poem "The Apology"
(Evening Street Press) was nominated for a Pushcart Prize in
2021.

www.ingramcontent.com/pod-product-compliance
Lightning Source LLC
Chambersburg PA
CBHW051337120626
46547CB00016B/2584